The need for
SPEED
Monster Trucks

6

Mike Johnstone

W
FRANKLIN WATTS

CREDITS

This edition published in 2002 by
Franklin Watts
96 Leonard Street
London EC2A 4XD

Franklin Watts Australia
45-51 Huntley Street
Alexandria
NSW 2015

Designed by: Jason Billin / Billin Design Solutions
Art director: Jonathan Hair
Editor in Chief: John C. Miles

A CIP catalogue record for this book
is available from the British Library

ISBN 0 7496 4753 1

Dewey Decimal Classification 796.7

Printed in Dubai

Picture credits: Front cover: Allsport UK Ltd,
(middle and bottom Tim DeFrisco) Back cover:
Allsport UK Ltd, pp. 1 main and inset, Andrew
Fielder, 2-3 left Andrew Fielder, middle Eric Stern,
right Andrew Fielder, 4-5 main and inset Andrew
Fielder, 6-7 main Allsport UK Ltd (Ron Hornaday)
inset Allsport UK Ltd (Kevin Cywinski), 8-9 main
(Mike Wallace), inset (Kevin Harvick), 10-11
Andrew Fielder, 12-13 Andrew Fielder, 14-15
Andrew Fielder, 16-17 Andrew Fielder, 18-19 Eric
Stern, 20-21 Eric Stern, 22-23 Andrew Fielder,
24-25 Andrew Fielder, 26-27 Eric Stern, 30-31 left
and middle Andrew Fielder, inset Allsport UK Ltd
(Kevin Cywinski)

CONTENTS

INTRODUCTION

If you have ever seen truck or monster truck racing live or on television, you may have wondered what it was like to sit in the cockpit of one of those amazing machines.

The Need for Speed puts you in the driver's seat of some of the most famous trucks in the game as they roar around a race track or thunder towards empty cars, about to turn them into a mass of tangled and twisted metal.

The trucks featured in this book include the granddaddy of them all, Bigfoot, which less than 25 years ago became the first monster car-crusher.

Since then, truck racing and monster trucking have taken off in a big way, especially in the United States where they are big business. The sports are gradually becoming more and more popular in other countries as well.

The vehicles may have different names, but all monster trucks have features in common. These include huge engines and tyres and The Need for Speed.

As well as giving you a taste of the thrills of truck racing and monster trucking, we also give you some facts and figures behind these incredible machines. These are found in the **Stat Files** and **Track Files**, which look like this.

STAT FILE

Black Stallion

Make:	Ford F150
Weight:	4549 kg (10,028 lbs)
Height:	3 m (10 ft)

NASCAR and ARCA truck racing

Realizing that there was a growing interest in truck racing, NASCAR (the National Association for Stock Car Auto Racing) first organized a few exhibition races in 1994. The response from fans was so positive that they sanctioned an entire season the following year. On seeing how popular the new sport was becoming, in 1998, ARCA (the Automobile Racing Club of America) decided to organize a couple of exhibition truck races of its own, and the following year added a full season of truck racing.

The Fact File gives you a slightly unusual, strange or funny bit of information.

FACT FILE

Expensive power

Monster truck engines are limited by rules to 9423 cc (575 ci). Custom-built for extra power, a decent one makes a hole of around £20,000 in a monster trucker's bank account!

NASCAR CRAFTSMAN TRUCKS

When NASCAR officials started to research the potential of truck racing as a spectator attraction, they were surprised at the strength of the response.

It wasn't long before a sponsor -– Craftsman Tools – came forward to put money into the sport. This allowed the creation of a new class of vehicle on the race circuit – NASCAR Craftsman trucks.

The trucks are built in modular style (with separate, easily replaceable body parts), are rear-wheel driven and are built to withstand rough, tough driving. But perhaps the trucks' main attraction to the people who race them is that they can do much of the maintenance themselves.

FACT FILE

The main difference between driving a Craftsman truck and a Winston Cup stock car is that the increased wheelbase affects chassis loading and weight distribution, making them quite a challenge to handle.

NASCAR rules stipulate that the trucks' engines must run on a 9:1 compression ratio, which limits the speed they can reach.

NASCAR CRAFTSMAN TRUCKS

With safety uppermost in their minds, there are many experts who want NASCAR's 9:1 compression rule to be applied across the stock racing board. The research being put into developing Craftsman trucks will be vital in deciding if this happens.

As well as being an exciting sport in its own right, NASCAR craftsman truck racing is excellent training for the Winston Cup stock car drivers of tomorrow.

A beginner who can put a truck through its paces in a NASCAR truck race is developing the skills that will enable him (or, increasingly, her) to take to the wheel of a Winston Cup stock car and power it round Daytona, Indianapolis or any of the tracks on the US NASCAR circuit.

Dubbed "supertruck racing", the sport gives would-be stock car drivers great experience.

FACT FILE

On to a winner

NASCAR's decision to back truck racing has paid off, not just in terms of increasing gate receipts at race tracks all over the United States, but because of the opportunities it gives for research and development, for example in trying new kinds of engine.

As well as NASCAR Craftsman truck racing and ARCA truck racing, there's monster truck racing – a sport that has thrilled thousands of Americans coast to coast for more than 25 years. The sport is now spreading to Britain, Sweden and other European countries.

It all started in the late 1970s when a number of pick-up fans started to experiment with ways of making their trucks bigger and better. One of the first to do so was Bob Chandler, who owned a business specializing in selling four-wheel-drive vehicles. Between 1976 and 1982, Bob added bigger and bigger tyres to his Ford F250 pick-up, improved its suspension and put in rear steering.

In 1981, as a way of publicizing his business, Chandler bought a couple of old wrecks from a local junkyard close to St. Louis, Missouri, and drove them to a nearby cornfield. He set up a video camera, revved up the engine of his hybrid pick-up, and sent it roaring towards the old jalopies. A few seconds later they were little more than a pile of compressed metal!

Bob put the video on a loop at his showroom and his customers loved it. In April 1982, an enterprising promoter persuaded Chandler to repeat the crush, this time in front of an audience. The crush took place in Jefferson, Missouri. Several thousand people paid to watch it. And a new sport was born: car crushing.

Today, truck fests are held all over the United States and, increasingly, in other countries. The regular appearances of monster trucks on television, especially satellite television, is starting to make monster trucking a popular sport all over the world.

SPEED . . .
AND SAFETY

Monster trucks are built for high-power bursts of speed. They generate between 1500 and 2000 hp and reach speeds of up to 160 km/h (100 mph).

In car-jump events, they can fly through the air for 35 metres (115 feet), and sometimes reach a height of 7.5 metres (25 feet).

Safety rules demand that each truck is fitted with three ignition interruptor switches, all of which are checked each time a truck comes up to the starting line, no matter how often that may be at any one event.

Drivers wear a five-point safety harness, neck collar, gloves and a fireproof suit.

The number of cars a monster has to jump in competition varies from stadium to stadium and depends on the length of the track, but generally, at indoor shows, drivers attempt to get their trucks over 18 cars and at outdoor events as many as 25 cars side-to-side. As with crush events, cars are usually bought from local scrapyards.

Most monster trucks have continuous fibreglass bodies with no door. The driver and any passengers climb into the cab through a manhole on the passenger-side floorboard.

After a jump, a truck can land with a bang . . .

. . . and roll over – but it's unlikely the driver will be hurt.

Staying safe

All monster trucks have, under competition rules, to be fitted with a minimum eight-point, steel roll cage and they must have an approved fire extinguisher system that the driver can operate with his or her eyes closed, in the seat-belted position. There must also be a firewall to protect the driver's compartment against an engine fire. Rules also specify that the windscreen should be made of a shatterproof material called Lexan.

WHAT A CRUSH

Most monster truck fests feature a mixture of events such as races, jumps and freestyle stunts, but what brings the audiences to their feet are car crushes.

The pre-crush events in full swing, the monster truck drivers zip themselves into their suits, clamber onto the tyres and pull themselves up into their cabins.

When the engines leap into life and the drivers put their trucks into gear, the trucks start to vibrate violently. They roar round the arena, the drivers performing wheelies and other tricks that show off their skills at the wheels of their four-by-four monsters.

Then the trucks get into position and wait for the green starting light. The first driver to go pulls his restraining straps tight and puts his foot down hard on the accelerator. The thrust generated by his massive engine pushes him back into his seat as his truck races towards the line of parked cars.

As impact occurs, the cars that were in the driver's sights vanish from his view as his front tyres crunch into them. Using every bit of his (or her) expertise, the driver raises the truck onto its back wheels like some prehistoric monster rearing up to devour its prey.

Seconds after the rear tyres crunch into the cars, the driver brings his truck crashing down, then races away. What was, a few moments before, a line of scrapped but still recognizable cars has become a sad pile of twisted metal, roofs slammed into floors, bumpers sticking out at odd angles, fragments of ripped upholstery flapping in the breeze. Then the rest of the drivers take their turns.

The crush over, it's time for the audience to make its way home and for the drivers to wind down, check their trucks for any damage and get ready for the next event – which may be hundreds of kilometres away.

FACT FILE

An expensive game

Running a monster truck costs money – big money. The vehicles have to be hauled from venue to venue and have to be maintained in tip-top condition. All this costs more than £80,000 a year.

For weeks before a truck fest, organizers scour scrapyards for old cars to crush.

BIGFOOT

In 1983 Bob Chandler's company arranged a sponsorship deal with Ford. Since then a total of 16 of his Bigfoot monster trucks have thrilled live spectators coast to coast in the United States and television audiences around the world.

It's not just Bigfoot that has benefited from the deal: since 1983, the Ford F series, on which Bigfoot is based, has become the world's best-selling truck, in no small measure due to the popularity of monster trucking.

Bigfoot became such a success that by 1985 more and more enthusiasts were starting to adapt their own trucks, making monsters out of production-line models; car crushes became bigger and bigger crowd-pullers.

Within a year or two, however, spectators started to demand something new, so monster truck owners started to race their amazing creations against one another and make their trucks take to the air over jumps.

This new phase of the sport quickly caught on, both at live events and when it was picked up by satellite and cable television companies.

Versatile Bigfoot is a favourite at crush events...

...and also at jumps and races all over the United States.

BEARFOOT CHEVROLET

Built in 1979, Bearfoot was one of the first monster trucks to take to the sporting scene.

Fred Shafer, the man who created it, was one of the top names in the sport until he retired in 1998. For 18 years Fred and his wife Kathy travelled all over the United States, entertaining audiences at major venues and smaller state fairs.

Shafer began his racing career on the Drag Racing circuit in 1965 when he was 18 years old and quickly established himself as one of the most competent of drivers. By the end of the 1970s he was keen to try his hand at something new, so he and a friend, Jack Willman, bought a 1979 Chevrolet powered pick-up truck, beefed up the frame and replaced the standard Chevrolet axles with five-tonne military ones. They also fitted the truck with monster-sized 1.66-metre (66-inch) Goodyear tyres.

Now weighing over eight tonnes, the truck was so successful that within 10 years (by which time Shafer's partnership with Willman had ended), seven more monster trucks had been added to the Bearfoot fleet.

STAT FILE

BEARFOOT CHEVROLET

Make:	Chevrolet
Weight:	8 tonnes/tons
Tyres:	1.66-m (66-in) Goodyear
Engine:	7466 cc (456 ci)
Suspension:	Heavy-duty leaf springs

Big jump

Fred Shafer entered the record books in 1996 when Bearfoot jumped just over 43 metres (141 feet). The record held for two years.

In 1991 Fred Shafer, who had built the Chevrolet-based Bearfoot team into one of the leaders in the world of monster trucks, realized that if his team was to stay at the top he needed more funds to finance future expansion.

After several months of secret negotiations, it was announced that Bearfoot was to abandon Chevrolet in favour of Dodge.

The first fruit of the Dodge/Shafer collaboration was Bearfoot 10, a fibreglass-bodied monster based on the Dodge Dakota pick-up. It was an immediate hit with Dodge dealers (who vied with each other to book the vehicle in their areas to promote their trucks) and spectators alike. It was a success on the race track, too – in 1992 the vehicle won the Camel World Championship. As with his Chevrolet-based Bearfoot, Shafer had a nail-biting wait – until the last race of the season – to find out that he had won the title.

The following year saw the introduction of Bearfoot 11, again based on the Dodge Dakota. The 9373 cc (572 ci) dry-block engine (one that has no coolant in it) gave 1500 hp and was positioned below the driver, about one metre (3.2 feet) off the ground – a new twist that caused many teething problems.

Dodge got their money's worth out of their sponsorship deal with Bearfoot. Fred Shafer's team clinched not only the World Championship title, but several world speed records as well.

STAT FILE

BEARFOOT DODGE

Make:	Dodge Dakota
Engine:	9373 cc (572 ci) dry-block, 1500 hp

FACT FILE

TV stars

Two trucks from Fred Shafer's stable featured in the 1980s TV series Knight Rider. They collided and appeared to burst into flames, courtesy of the TV studio's special effects department.

BLACK STALLION 2000

Maryland monster trucker Mike Vater drove into the new millennium in a updated version of his highly rated Black Stallion called Black Stallion 2000.

Built around a 1997 Ford F150 pick-up, Black Stallion 2000 has four-link suspension with custom-built sway bars, Rockwell 106 axles and 1.66-metre (66-inch) tyres.

From cabin top to tyre bottom, Black Stallion 2000 stands 3 metres (10 feet) high and is 3.66 metres (12 feet) wide.

Some drivers take a leap over two dozen cars in their stride. At a four-wheel-drive jamboree in Philadelphia, Mike Vater went one better. He jumped over another monster truck – Andy Hoffman's Nitemare!

To pull off a trick like that and come down to earth without too much of a bang, a truck needs an awesome suspension. Black Stallion 2000 gets it from a KS Nitro Shock Suspension system – the best in the business. The shocks are fully adjustable to vehicle weight and ride height. They work in each direction of travel through hydraulic valving and need no other mechanical springs.

At over 4,500 kg (9,900 lbs) Black Stallion is a real crusher.

A thrilling moment as Black Stallion flies over Nitemare.

Black Stallion

Make:	Ford F150
Weight:	4549 kg (10,028 lbs)
Height:	3 m (10 ft)

EXECUTIONER

Based in Illinois and owned and driven by brothers Tim and Mark Hall, Executioner is a great crowd-puller at monster truck fests.

Tim Hall is one of monster trucking's most influential players, having been President of the Monster Truck Racing Association from 1997. Executioner was in the top five trucks in both the 1996 PENDA points series and the following year's Special Events Points Series. It was named truck of the year in 1996, the same year that the Halls were awarded most improved team of the year, and Mark Hall driver of the year.

The truck is a 1990 Dodge Ram pick-up powered by a 8439 cc (515 ci) supercharged, alcohol-burning engine that delivers 1000 hp. The Lenco air-shift transmission permits smooth gear changing and the 8KS nitrogen shock absorbers coupled with the four-link suspension give the driver a smooth ride. The Hall Brothers built the tubular racing chassis themselves. The massive Goodyear Terra tyres are more than half-a-metre deep.

EXECUTIONER

FACT FILE

Expensive monster

Like all vehicles registered with the Monster Truck Racing Association, Executioner has a certified value for insurance purposes – $110,000 US.

STAT FILE

Executioner

Make:	Dodge Ram
Engine:	8439 cc (515 ci) alcohol-burning

KING KRUNCH

When it comes to crushing cars, King Krunch lives up to its name as the 60,000 fans who crammed into the Houston Astrodome in January 2000 will testify.

That was the night when 16 of the top names in monster trucking thundered onto the field to compete against each other. At the end of the night it was King Krunch that reigned supreme.

The truck is owned and driven by Scott Stephens, from Spring, in Texas. Scott has been driving monster trucks since 1980. He was among the first drivers to experiment with turbine-powered aircraft engines in monster trucks. This kind of engine makes flames shoot out from under the bonnet, delighting spectators.

Today's King Krunch is based on a 1999 Dodge Ram pick-up and is powered by a 9373 cc (572 ci) engine. It is proving to be very successful. Apart from its triumph at Houston, it was third at the Pace Motor Sports Monster Trucking World Finals in Las Vegas. In the 2000 USHRA monster truck circuit, King Krunch regularly featured in the top ten competing trucks.

In monster trucking language, this manoeuvre is called a "sky wheelie".

STAT FILE

King Krunch

Make:	1999 Dodge Ram
Engine:	9373 cc (572 ci)

SAMSON

As befits a vehicle named after the biblical strongman, Dan Patrick's monster truck has strength in abundance.

Weighing in at almost five tonnes and powered by a 9225 cc (563 ci) hemispherical engine, the truck has a Chevrolet Silverado body and is equipped with four-speed Lenco air-shift transmission. It has two nitrogen-charged shock absorbers fitted to each of its four wheels. Giant Goodyear tyres complete Samson's monstrous appearance.

Dan Patrick was just 17 when he started to compete in motor sports, beginning with tractor-pulling competitions in and around his home town of Kingston, Ohio.

In 1988 he and his newly built Samson entered the world of monster trucks when he joined United Sports of America's Motor Spectacular. He made such an impact that the following year he was approached by the Bigfoot team to contribute to the design of the next generation of monster trucks.

▼ When two trucks race in such a spectacular style, it's little wonder the crowd gets excited! .

29

FACT FILE

Moving the monster
Samson features at more
than 100 truck fests a year. It is
transported from show to
show on a custom-built
transporter that comes equipped
with living quarters and
a repair shop.

If you are keen on truck or monster truck racing, here are some names and numbers that might be useful.

The British Truck Racing Association
c/o Sparshotts of Kent
Unit 10, Eurolink Industrial Estate
Sittingbourne
Kent ME10 3RN
Tel: 01795 479571

Automobile Racing Club of America
PO Box 5215
Toledo
Ohio
OH 4361
Tel: 313 847 6726

NASCAR
PO Box 2875
Daytona Beach
Florida
FL 32120
Tel: 904 253 0611
Fax: 904 252 8804
Email: publicrelations@nascar.com
www.nascar.com

Professional Racing Organization
PO Box 4327
Portsmouth
New Hampshire
NH 03802
Tel: 603 433 8448

Rally Race Trucks
PO Box 1136
Coshocton
Ohio
OH 43812
Tel: 614 622 7316

Short Track Super Trucks
PO Box 3227
Chilton
Wisconsin
WI 53014
Tel: 414 849 7036

WEBSITES TO VISIT

Andrew Fielder's Monster Trucks
www.monstertruck-uk.com

Bigfoot 4 x 4 www.bigfoot4x4.com

Fourwheeler Magazine Online
www.fourwheeler.com

Eric Stern
www.monstertruckracing.com

Gun Slinger Monster Truck
www.gunslinger4x4.com

Jurassic Attack Monster Truck
www.jurassicattack.com

Mike's Monster Trucks
www.mikesmonstertrucks.com

Rampage Monster Truck www.wko.com

Sudden Impact Monster Truck
www.suddenimpact.com

Special Events: The Promotion Company
www.familyevents.com

Truckworld www.truckworld.com

US Hot Rod Association
www.ushra.com

Anyone who has ever been to a monster truck event and has overheard drivers chatting to each other may begin to wonder what on earth they were talking about. Here are some of the words they use:

Bite Traction.

Burn out/dry hop To spin the truck's tyres to clear them of mud and gain bite.

Cut tyres To shave the tread off the tyres to gain bite or lose weight.

Donut When a truck spins circles in one spot in the arena.

Eyeball the track To inspect the track or competition.

Good lookin' clay Track dirt that makes it easy for the tyres to hook up.

Grab a footful Jumping on the accelerator.

Grenade launch To damage an engine or other truck part especially badly.

Hole shot First vehicle off the starting line.

Hook up To dig in the tyres and take off fast from the starting line.

Hot shoe A top driver.

Lose fire Stall the engine.

Pogo When a truck comes down hard and bounces back up with the rear end hitting the ground over and over again.

Pull the pin When a truck rolls over, the emergency pin in the rear bumper is pulled to shut off the power.

Power out When a driver uses a burst of acceleration to keep his truck from rolling.

Red light When a truck leaves the starting line early, before the green starting light.

Sky wheelie When a truck rolls up to an object in the arena and hits it hard with the front tyres, causing the rear end to stand straight up.

Teeter When a driver wheelies the front end with the rear tyres on the ground and causes the truck to teeter from side to side.

Tranny The transmission that transfers power from the engine to the drive train.

Wheelie The ability to get the truck up on its rear wheels, lifting the front off the ground.

INDEX